# ICONS OF THE INCARNATION

## SOPHIE HACKER

Meditations by
## ROLAND RIEM

CANTERBURY
PRESS
Norwich

For my family

© Sophie Hacker 2008

Further examples of Sophie Hacker's work
and other details can be found on
www.sophiehacker.com

First published in 2008 by the Canterbury Press Norwich
(a publishing imprint of Hymns Ancient & Modern Limited,
a registered charity)
13-17 Long Lane, London EC1A 9PN

www.scm-canterburypress.co.uk

Picture credits: Photographs of the artworks and their details © Joe Low;
Sarah Baldock and Sophie Hacker (p. 4) © Abha Thakor 2007;
the great organ at Winchester cathedral (p. 54) © Winchester Diocesan Board;
other pictures are the author's own copyright, or copyright sought for
those as yet unknown

British Library Cataloguing in Publication data

A catalogue record for this book is available
from the British Library

ISBN 978-1-85311-926-2

Printed and bound by BAS Printers

# FOREWORD
by Richard Harries

I was fortunate in being able to view Sophie Hacker's exhibition when it was first on show in Winchester Cathedral. Although it was conceived in response to music by Messiaen, and the first viewing was in conjunction with that music, it struck me that the art work stands very well on its own. Now it is good to have Sophie's own account of how she came to produce this work and what it means to her. It is also good to have Roland Riem's lapidary poetic meditations for each of the icons.

Sophie brings out how important are found objects (*objets trouvé*) to these icons. Each one comes with a past history, which is why, except with some copper off-cuts, she does not alter them; but each is fully integrated into a total scheme of geometry, colour, texture and shape.

Much modern art leaves people baffled or disdainful. Yet it is also clear that so much art that goes on sale at a more popular level is no more than what Constable termed 'eye salve'. Sophie avoids this polarization. Her work is I believe very accessible, for example the icon of 'The Angels', but it repays prolonged looking, as in 'Jesus accepts suffering'.

Sophie trained as an abstract painter but has increasingly come to see sculpture as her main medium. When these two elements come together as in these works in low relief, and are combined with her powerful unifying use of colour, the results both communicate and suggest that which cannot finally be communicated. This is another reason why these icons are helpful today. Any form of Literalism in religion, whether in words or pictures, is totally inadequate to convey the mystery of God and therefore does a great disservice to a true understanding of religion. But Christianity claims that the Word became flesh, that God has made himself accessible to us in and through a human life. The problem both for the preacher and artist working on Christian themes from the standpoint of faith is how to share both the mystery of what cannot be made known and what has been made known. These works on the Incarnation celebrate the coming among us of the Divine Life. But they make it clear that this Divine Life, being Divine, is beyond anything we can finally grasp in human terms.

I think people will enjoy both contemplating the icons in this book and reading how they have come about and what they mean to their maker.

Professor Lord Harries of Pentregarth
Former Bishop of Oxford

1

# INTRODUCTION

In the spring of 2007, I began a project that was to absorb my working life for the following nine months. What made the project special was the opportunity to combine three art forms – music, painting and poetry. Like all the best adventures, I wasn't sure at the start where it would take me, or what I would discover on the way. Having reached the journey's end, it has brought me further than anticipated.

I grew up in a family where music was part of the furniture. My parents met as music students: my father is a clarinet soloist and conductor. My sister is also musical, but I found myself much more drawn to the visual.

I began to make pictures and model in plasticine or clay as a very small child, and I never really stopped. Abandoning myself to creative projects has provided a wonderful alternative world to inhabit – a place where I can feel more keenly, think more clearly and value what comes out of the process.

Colour has always been a crucial part of my work. For some years, I used soft, chalky pastels to create abstract and semi-abstract images, (such as 'Ekstasis' seen here). Putting down many layers of pigment I was able to build up rich textures.

'Ekstasis' (pastel on paper)
Private collection.

In recent years my work has become more sculptural. I have been using 'found' objects and materials since 2001, when I took up the post of artist-in-residence at Sarum College, a unique place of learning and study in Salisbury's Cathedral Close. The proximity of my studio there to the stonemason's yard proved very inspiring. I began to work with whatever materials came to hand around the cathedral precincts, looking for ways to energize them with new purpose and meaning – pieces of stone worked by masons and then discarded, slabs of alabaster from long-dismantled tombs or memorials, piles of weathered Chilmark stone that would have once formed part of the original cathedral building.

My studio has gradually filled up with interesting rubbish, liberated from skips, unearthed on muddy walks with the dog, rescued from the waves on beaches. I can't explain

'Pilgrim', made essentially from three pieces of wood with a stone base. The wood was gathered over a period of four years. Once they were all in the studio I then discovered what they would become. I added leather and fibres, paint and verdigris to complete the work.

what defines a piece 'worth' taking. Sometimes I know instantly what it will become; the head of a pilgrim, the arm for a Corpus, part of an abstracted landscape. At other times, it has taken some years for the object to find its home.

What all the found objects have in common is that they bear evidence of some past history. Wood adrift in the seas, now weathered and shaped by water, hard edges and splinters worn away. Shards of abandoned metal once made for a practical purpose, now broken and rusted to uselessness. These are the things that interest me. It excites me to give new life to these rejected elements, and constantly amazes me how so often when just exactly that shape, colour or material is needed for a project – there it is! To the right is a photograph showing four sides of the same sculpture, simply a very worn remnant from Salisbury Cathedral's cloisters, probably shaped during the mediaeval period. For me it is charged with history and significance, even though it was discarded by the masons. I have gilded it with the words from St Paul's letter to the Romans: 'For when I am weak, then I am strong.' The verse neatly sums up my theology of using 'found materials'.

Using unpredictable materials in making my work brings a range of technical challenges; how to attach shards of glass to soft fabric, how to gild a tortuously twisted piece of driftwood. By working across the disciplines of painter, sculptor and refuse collector, I have found new ways of making art that are endlessly rewarding and immensely enjoyable. The Messiaen Project challenged me to develop and refine many of these techniques, some of which I will be exploring later.

## THE MESSIAEN PROJECT

In January 2007 Sarah Baldock, then Assistant Director of Music at Winchester Cathedral, approached me about a collaborative project combining art and music. Her idea was to explore the score of Olivier Messiaen's *La Nativité du Seigneur* with an artist, somehow to make visible the images she saw when playing the piece's nine organ movements. The works would be exhibited in Winchester Cathedral as she and Andrew Lumsden performed the suite for the Feast of the Epiphany 2008. Roland Riem, a canon at Winchester Cathedral (and my husband), was

Some of my store of found materials

'For when I am weak, then I am strong'. (Chilmark stone, perspex, bole colour, 22 carat gold leaf) Private collection

Detail of 'Hospitality' (Chilmark stone, pigment, gold leaf, textile) Collection of Sarum College Inspired by the truly wonderful 'Hospitality of Abraham' by Rublev, I used three pieces of Chilmark stone, with the three colours used in icon painting to represent the three persons of the Trinity. I talk about this language of 'sacred colour' later in the book.

3

invited to write poetic meditations drawing together the music and the artworks. These meditations were to be read at the performance and are published here for the first time, alongside the full image of each of their corresponding art works.

I had some initial reservations, having found some of Messiaen's music fairly unapproachable. However, listening to a variety of recordings of this piece, and sitting next to Sarah in the organ loft, watching her play it, my response to the music changed completely. Like Sarah, I also found strong visual images coming to mind. Some of the movements are more descriptive than others –'The Virgin and Child', 'The Angels', 'The Magi', 'The Shepherds' – these all have a rich, long life in art history. Others – 'The Children of God', 'Eternal Designs' – defy an easy translation into visual images.

Sarah and I began to meet and discuss the score. How interesting that she, as a musician, should talk predominantly about the colours and pictures she saw in the music, while I, as a visual artist, found myself increasingly drawn to the sounds and structure of the composition.

We discovered early on that our theological outlooks were sympathetic, and we could work with Messiaen's personal vision of faith. His stated intention in writing *La Nativité* was to honour the Virgin, while I found myself more drawn to its incarnational themes.

It would be impossible to extricate my faith from my art. One informs the other in constant conversation, with my belief at the heart of what I do. I seldom use explicitly Christian iconography in my studio work, since I normally use a more abstract language, though I have made crosses, crucifixes and figurative icons for churches, chapels or private devotions. One of the exciting aspects of this collaboration was the chance to explore Messiaen's deeply considered, theological imagery without the need to become too literal in its representation.

As we explored the score, I began to sketch the shapes and note textures and colours that emerged. The theology implicit in the music was always to the fore; affirming, human, full of images of love and sacrifice, and teeming with joyful, sometimes overwhelming passion.

Most of the movements contain several themes, and often the challenge was to acknowledge that not all of them could be conveyed in just one artwork devoted to that movement. Sarah and I agreed on which ones to include

Sarah Baldock (left) and I discuss the score in the studio

4

and which to omit, because my intention was not to try to 'illustrate' the music. Roland Riem's meditations draw out some of the themes we weren't able to include, giving a more rounded account of the music. He speaks about these on page 7.

When we had been through the score several times, I set off to find the right pigments and materials to realize the artwork. Only a few of the elements I would need were already in the studio; most had yet to be discovered. I went on many scavenging trips to beaches and forests and found new places to explore, such as scrap metal yards and glass works.

Sketching shapes and textures from the music

One particularly useful meeting was with Steve, a steel fabricator from the New Forest. He showed me how to shape and cut copper, which became a significant element in several of the pieces. With the exception of the copper (off-cuts I had been given from a roofing project at Sarum College some years ago), all the found objects I use remain structurally unchanged. I will add colour, and sometimes texture, but I always aim to use the object as I find it. If it's the wrong size, I rarely cut it down or re-shape it. This seems very important, as a way to honour the history the object brings with it.

The works are not icons in the Orthodox sense, which use specific visual forms. However, they have their own symbolic language, which likewise aims to create a window into the divine. Every aspect, whether material, colour or shape, carries a meaning that is relevant to the narrative. Some of these draw on traditional understandings, such as the language of colour in sacred art. Others evolved in the process of making. I'll be drawing attention to this symbolic language as I talk about each piece in turn.

I needed a physical framework within which to explore this rich and multi-layered music. After all, Messiaen himself had the framework of one instrument, the organ, although it has many different voices. I began with a basic 30-inch square and decided to work on thick wooden panels, which would give the necessary strength to the processes that would be inflicted on the surface – cutting, drilling, nailing, sanding. I began to see how the works would need to be shown, each having a separate, individuated space to inhabit, yet linked with every other piece. The sacred geometry of the equilateral triangle emerged as the right solution for this. This simple shape has been a perfect symbol of the Trinity for centuries, representing each person of the Trinity as having equal authority and significance.

I built three triangular wooden pillars, which were placed at the three points of a larger, equilateral triangle in the North Transept of Winchester Cathedral. One artwork was placed on the three sides of each. Lit from above, striking patterns of shadow unexpectedly emerged. I found these really beautiful, and was surprised at the way the shadows helped to emphasize the physical space created by the large, outer triangle shape.

The beauty of this structure is that it immediately creates an interior space, in which to place the 'nativity' images (virgin and child, shepherds and angels), as well as a space to journey around the works, weaving between the columns, following the story that Messiaen sketches out for us.

During the Epiphany performance of *La Nativité*, films of each of the nine artworks were projected on to a large screen, thanks to Matt Blyth and Kate Beal of KMB Productions. They also made a short documentary on the making of the art.

In the following pages the nine images are explored. Each section starts with the biblical quotation, either a single text or amalgams of verses from Old and New Testaments. These quotes are of Messiaen's choosing and construction, and provided his initial inspiration for the music of *La Nativité*.

View from above the installation, North Transept, Winchester Cathedral

## THE MUSIC

### Sarah Baldock writes:

Olivier Messiaen is one of the most important composers for organ, and possibly stands alongside J. S. Bach in the extent and content of his output. Just as Bach's works are deeply rooted in the Christian faith, so Messiaen sought to expound theological concepts in much of his music. As a Christian musician working for Winchester Cathedral, it was my desire to perform one of Messiaen's suites, within the setting of the ancient Cathedral, and to add a visual element to the music. Many people find Messiaen's music difficult and modern, but presented alongside images, perhaps the sounds would make more sense. I was also interested in looking at different ways in which the theological concepts identified by Messiaen could be communicated.

*La Nativité* is a sequence of nine meditations on the birth of Christ. Each movement is prefaced with biblical quotations. Messiaen uses unconventional combinations of sounds on the organ, and covers a full range of emotions and dynamics, constantly evoking colour and images in the music. Some movements deal with particular characters in the Christmas story – 'The Virgin and Child', 'The Shepherds', 'The Angels', 'The Magi' – and they are given life in the music. 'Jesus Accepts Suffering' is a very graphic piece in which one can almost hear the crucifixion. The movements that deal with more conceptual ideas – 'Eternal Designs', 'The Word', 'The Children of God', 'God Among Us' – also tell a compelling story, and the music plays an interpretative role in the face of some meaty theology.

I wanted to find an artist with whom I could work to create nine pieces of art to stand alongside the music and the text. Sophie Hacker had the kind of gut reaction to the music that enabled a remarkable response to the textures and depictions inherent in Messiaen's work. The event that brought together the exhibition, performance of the suite, film presentation and Roland Riem's poetry, attracted an audience that comprised artists, church-goers, organ aficionados, general music-lovers and others. Each seemed to find a way into less-familiar areas in the interaction of the different art forms. The art and poetry that initially grew out of Messiaen's music have a strong independent impact.

## THE MEDITATIONS

**Roland Riem writes:**
The meditations are brief, unfussy introductions to the conversation between artist and organist envisaged by the Messiaen Project. Their style has to be simple enough to allow listeners to catch most of the meaning in one hearing, like hymns with a good metre and short verses – poetic and direct.

I began as Sophie did, by listening to each movement of *La Nativité* over and over again, in various recordings. I noted down any words and phrases that came to mind to develop a palette of ideas for each meditation. I also read the notes Sophie had made in preparation for her icons. By this point I knew those images well, though I tried always to return to the music as the common source of inspiration.

Sometimes the meditations make an obvious musical reference: 'carolling with quickening pace' ('The Shepherds') or 'the surge and slip of sound' ('Eternal Designs'). Sometimes the meditation picks up on pitch: 'spiralling, they circle low' ('The Angels'), or it captures the mood of the music: 'a dazzling whirligig of joy' ('God Among Us'). Sometimes the thrust of the verse reflects the musical dynamics: the first stanza of 'The Children of God' echoes the climactic ascent at the beginning of that movement; 'Eternal Designs' is one sentence long just as the music is only one page long.

The images themselves cannot be ignored for long, though. The weathered rib of wood central to the icon of 'Jesus Accepts Suffering' dominates the poetic landscape – 'splintered right', 'knotted and gnarled', 'the grain of wrong', 'a door', 'a stair', 'the world's wood is turned'. And yet the music still provides the narrative in which these metaphors are framed: at the beginning a harsh call from God is sounded. By the end of the movement Christ's body on the cross converts injustice into triumphant redemption. It is tough to couple art and music into one short meditation, and all the harder because poems and carols crowd the mind as soon as one starts writing nativity verse. Well-worn words like angels, joy, peace and praise need to be used sparingly, though they can scarcely be avoided!

I hope not to have been too derivative, but I gratefully acknowledge the influence of my favourite poet Gerard Manley Hopkins who above all other modern poets, in my view, knew how words swung in combination and proper order.

As Sophie made each of her nine icons the same size, I decided to follow suit by making each meditation fourteen lines long. It was comforting to be in touch, however obliquely, with the tradition of sonnets, those great vehicles for expressing the breadth and depth of love.

If anyone wishes to use these meditations publicly, please do; but say them as slowly as you dare, and then probably slower still. Feel the gaps between the lines, between words, and sometimes even between syllables, such as the five of 'unfathomably'. The meditations are short so that you can dwell on them and help others into the truth beyond – the great mystery of God among us in Christ.

# THE VIRGIN AND CHILD

Conceived by a Virgin a Child is born to us,
a Son has been given to us.
Rejoice greatly, O daughter of Zion!
Lo, your king comes to you, just and lowly.

What calm the newborn brings!

In her arms
In intensity of love
He rests.

But her heart's contentment
Spreads, till the whole of womankind
Rings out and sings, Nativity.

This One is here.
Lovable and low,
A king and child in time,
A cursor to eternity.

And now a mother's eye looks down,
And here two open souls entwine,
As touch and tenderness uphold him.

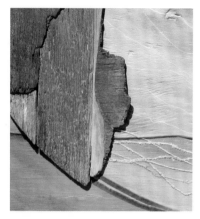

The lower edge of the 'mother'

Our Lady of St Theodore, showing the use of burgundy red. Russian icons are more likely to clothe the Virgin in red

The simplicity at the heart of the Nativity inspired this image. Rough wood provides a home for the two central forms. The soft brown hues in this wooden background are traditionally associated with an earthy humility, and here represent the stable. The two central forms representing the virgin and her infant, are also made from wood, parts of a plywood cable reel (the sort of thing that students take out of skips to make into a coffee table). The cable reel had lain for years outside some allotments in Salisbury. I had watched it change and decay over time, until, once this project began, I knew that its moment had come!

The 'head' of the smaller, child, piece originally nestled perfectly against the lower edge of the large piece, so in a sense, this mother had truly given birth to her infant. I worked on the surface of the wood to draw out its grain and weathered textures. Both forms have the traditional colours associated with Christ and Mary, that of ultramarine blue, red (here a rich, burgundy hue) and white. Ultramarine, which means 'coming from beyond the sea', was first used around the sixth century AD, in Afghanistan. It is produced from lapis lazuli, a rare mineral pigment. Not only is the very best lapis extremely hard to come by, but the process of extracting the pigment is lengthy and expensive, creating a large amount of waste. As a result, ultramarine was the most expensive material for artists, even more costly than gold leaf. Even today, prices are in excess of £2,500 for 500gm of Afghan Ultramarine, made to a traditional recipe. The cost inevitably added to its significance as a colour in icon painting, and was reserved for painting the Virgin and Christ's robes. Nowadays, most ultramarine is produced as a synthetic pigment, which makes it affordable, though perhaps loses some of its romantic history in the process.

Lapis lazuli

12

Renaissance artists used these three colours for their theological meaning, but for centuries before and after that time, icon painters also used them for the Virgin and Christ. Blue is divine nature, revelation and the nature of God. Red, by contrast, symbolizes human nature, physical suffering, martyrdom. These opposites are brought together in Christ. White is the colour of purity and innocence. By sharing these three colours this mother and child become reflections of each other. Christ is divine, and embraces humanity, while Mary is human, but accepts divinity into her body in her child.

The virgin is also 'clothed' using a variety of embroidery threads, a technique I also use in 'The Magi' and 'The Shepherds' to indicate that these forms represent human personalities.

The child wears swaddling of wire, harsh and cutting, hinting at what lies ahead.

The wire on the 'child' form

The outer edges of these two shapes once formed part of a perfect circle. The circle is a universal symbol of unity, completeness and, again, of the divine. I've remade that circle using lead lines bedded into the wood. (Lead is used in several of the pieces. As a dull, heavy metal, it stands for the instruments of the passion – nails, mallets, pliers). The lead circle brings the two forms together, and creates an intimate embrace. There is the gentle sense of a rocking movement, the tender way a mother comforts and nurtures her child.

Lead circle and thread work

Contained within the circle is a shimmering passage of bright light colour, which seems to have great depth. Delicate threads echo the circle and weave a dance between the two forms. It speaks of the joy shared by the two, a joy that we are invited to enter and become part of.

13

# THE SHEPHERDS

Having seen the Babe lying in the manger,
the shepherds returned,
glorifying and praising God.

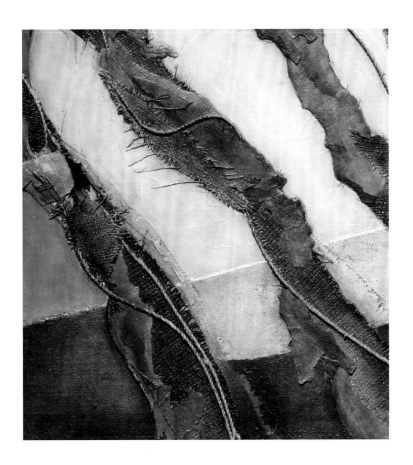

Wonderment slows their steps,
Draws them back where time
Lay penned in stillness.

In mind, they see the Lamb
Still wet against his mother's flank
Breathing the night-crisp air as they stand in light.

Yet now, their feet
Slowly catching what their fingers play,
Return them to their fold,
And carolling with quickening pace
They praise and celebrate
What God in grace has done

To bring the brake on ordinary ways
And shepherd them to heaven's gate.

The textures in the shepherd forms

I've mentioned earlier that brown hues traditionally represent earthiness and humility. In 'The Shepherds' various shades of brown are evident. These shepherds are 'earthed' and grounded. The browns also signify the transience of things bounded by our world, where everything created will also perish. Brown is not present on the colour wheel, which begins with the primary colours of red, blue and yellow, but it is an essential addition to an artist's palette, particularly to show the transition from dark to light. Walk around the Tuscan countryside and you will see shades of sienna winking at you from the ground. Siennas and umbers are truly straight from the earth. No wonder browns are given the role of humility in colour symbolism.

We see five forms marching across an upward-sloping landscape. This rising horizon is an important symbol in the work, and is also found in 'The Children of God', 'The Angels', 'The Magi', and in complement in 'The Word'. It stands for creation; the stuff of earth that we are all bounded by, which is also a wonderful gift.

I needed to find materials that were as natural and unprocessed as possible to reflect the shepherds' simplicity and connection with the earth. I gathered bark from local woods, found scraps of leather, old hessian sacking and rough hand-made papers, all of which were built up to a deeply textured surface, unified by umbers, siennas and terracotta colours. The pigments I painted them with are the same as the ones used to depict the earth they walk on. Thick, rope-like strings weave from top to bottom of each figure, perhaps like the crooks they would carry. The frayed fibres of hessian may be the edges of well-worn cloaks to keep out the chill of early morning. They are at one with their surroundings, part of the landscape they live on.

Messiaen responds similarly to these men of dust and rock. Musical phrases that one can describe as 'clunky' stomp through the movement. You can hear the honesty of their response, fired by their encounter in the stable, followed by joy as they turn back to the world and their working lives. *La Nativité du Seigneur* is acknowledged as 'programme music', which means it was written with the explicit intention of evoking ideas beyond purely musical ones. So images, moods, even a narrative, will form in the mind of the listener. In essence, programme music is designed to tell a story.

The blue beyond the central circle reads clearly as sky. It must be early in the morning, the first glimpse of dawn light just spreading up from the edge of the earth. This imminent surge of light is symbolic of the incarnation, and you will find it again in 'The Angels', 'The Children of God' and 'God Among Us'.

The shepherds are carrying an echo from the first image – the circle, here more sketchy and less formed, brings some of the light we see in 'The Virgin and Child'. A familiar tracery of threads like the ones in the first image dance around the inside of this rough circle too.

The shepherds are taking this light, and this dance, back out with them, not to hold on to it but to share it. Their feet carry them urgently back into the world, 'glorifying and praising God', though their heads and hearts are yearning to stay by the manger where they can be wrapped in the light and warmth of their encounter with the Christ-child and his mother.

Sky and circle

# ETERNAL DESIGNS

God, in his love, has predestined us to be
his adopted children, through Jesus Christ,
to the praise of his glorious grace.

From nothing stirs his first embrace –
Like some great tide of peace,
Each wave-shift swells, gathers for an age,
And settles to its proper place;

Nothing yet stands before its path –
No crash or fall against a rock,
No break against the shore of day
Is yet discerned;

Just the surge and slip of sound –
The step of ancient Wisdom's work,
The surety of Love's intent –
Extends through aeons
Unfathomably
In one unending phrase.

Experimenting with glazes

This image caused me the most grief, and was made and re-made at least four times over a six-month period. What a vast subject to attempt to depict in a space not much more than 30-inch square - nothing less than the unending, and eternal purposes of God, and his work in Christ! Messiaen's own approach to the theme is a great, pulsating flow of sound. My initial response to this music was to recall images I had seen from that amazing orbiting eye, the Hubble telescope. It has brought us incredible visions of galaxies and stars being born and exploding, far beyond the scope of our imagination. The true colours of these events and heavenly bodies can only be guessed at, but these composite photographs are as close as possible to what we would see if we could travel through space and look at them with our own eyes. I've often been struck by how cool these images from deep space often appear, accentuating their remoteness.

I started to lay down many layers of resin particles, a specialist artists' medium that I hoped would gradually give depth to the finished image. The layers were applied in waves, spilling over each other, gradually lifting away from the flatness of the panel.

After a week or so of building up these resin layers, I began to work with colour, choosing permanent rose and indanthrene blues in transparent glazes, to give a soft purplish colour with a touch of warmth to it. Washes of turquoise and a special iridescent medium were used to add coolness, depth and light. (By coincidence, I recently heard that astronomers broadly now agree that when our universe was first born, at the time of the Big Bang, its colour would have been turquoise!) There are also some touches of very finely ground gold coming from the outer edge of the central square motif.

24    It was essential to make reference to Christ – the

Word – in this image. One of my favourite parts of the Eucharistic liturgy is 'he opened wide his arms for us on the cross'. The crucifixion is, to me, the consummate act of love, where Christ reveals the depth and breadth of God's eternal purposes for us. So now, instead of the wooden beam standing for the instrument of death, it becomes the wide-open arms of acceptance and invitation. The outer edges of this beam lift away from the surface, into our space, as if at the start of an embrace. Lead lines are used, as in 'The Virgin and Child', to evoke the Passion.

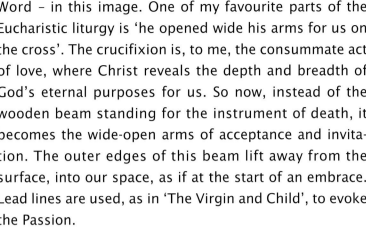

Outer edge of beam, showing the movement outwards towards the viewer

Messiaen 'saw' the quality of light through stained glass when writing this movement. He had a gift called 'synaesthesia', in which sounds, particularly musical ones, are experienced visually as well as aurally. The methods I used in these works could never replicate that 'stained glass' quality, but I hoped at least to hint at it, using three columns of Perspex, lifted slightly away from the surface to allow light to reach behind them, and tinted with careful washes of cobalt, rose, and a touch of turquoise, the colour of the young universe.

I was trying to combine a sense of background depth and spaciousness with a strong foreground presence of embrace and closeness. God is at once immanent and transcendent, closer than breath yet more vast than the deepest reaches of space. I could probably fruitfully spend the rest of my life trying to make a single piece of work that could encompass something of that, but after several struggles, I resolved this piece as best I could, and in a way that I felt connected with the music.

Perspex panel floating over the textured surface

# THE WORD

The Lord has said to me, 'You are my Son.'
From his breast, before creation's dawn,
he has begotten me. I am the Image of
the Goodness of God. I am the Word of Life,
from the beginning.

Out of goodness, wrought from might,
Life finds passage through which to pass
And labour's sweated pant and squeeze
Progresses on a cosmic stage.

The uttered Word, in might descends
Pressing His weight into soil and space,
His majesty, his granite strength,
Abandoning the Father's womb.

Beyond the breach, a winding song:
Love consoles that loss is meant;
Spirit affirms that flesh is blessed.

So comes delight upon the Son
Like fingers cupped around a face,
Till earth is staved in warmth and peace.

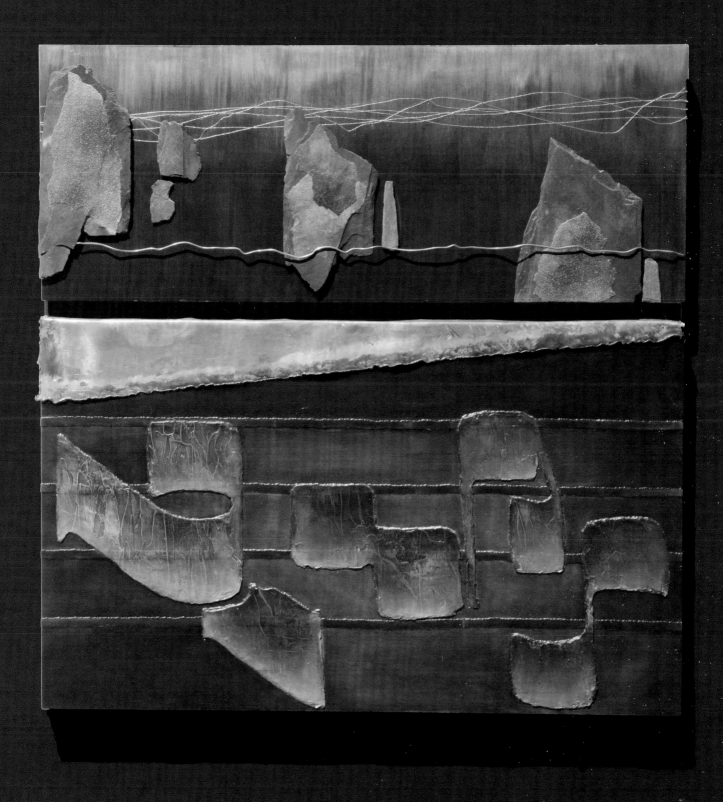

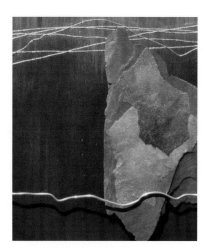

Slate, copper wire and gold threads

Detail of a neume shape

Two very different musical passages make up 'The Word'. The first is a powerful short section, which announces God's entrance into our world. Christ is the bridge that unites us with God, inhabiting both eternity and the present moment. Messiaen points to that bridge using the change between the two sections of music. After a pause, the music changes dramatically and becomes very quiet, slow and meditative. I've echoed those two sections by making my image in two separate pieces, joined by a hidden panel behind, painted very simply in pure graphite pigment. I also use similar colours, though very different textures, in both sections.

I needed to find materials that carried something rock-like and lasting. Three slabs of slate I found some years ago at the New Art Centre in Wiltshire fitted the bill perfectly. They march down the top section of the image, and have been enriched with colours and texture that began life in 'Eternal Designs'.

Running across them is an undulating line of copper, which emerges from behind the first slate, and disappears behind the far edge of the panel. It traces the journey as the slates descend, and symbolizes a sustained musical chord.

Above the tops of the slates are delicate golden threads. Gold is the most important colour in the hierarchy of sacred art, because unlike pigment, it reflects back pure light and colour in equal measure. Large areas of gold leaf can often be found in the background of Orthodox icons, to remove them from linear time and place them in eternal glory. A tracery of gold lines will also sometimes be rendered on Christ's robes to emphasize his divinity.

The lower section of this image is quite different in nature from the top, though there is an echo of many of the same colours. I mentioned earlier the symbol of the rising horizon used in images such as 'The Shepherds' and 'The Angels'. Here it is in complement – this time a panel of copper forms the part above the incline. I have used the copper in these works in the way I perhaps might have used gold, if I could have afforded it! Like gold it can also reflect light and energy, while having its own inherent tonality.

Beneath the copper panel, four ragged lead lines could be interpreted as staves, the lines used to hold the information needed to write and perform music. Instead of standard musical notation, the shapes they contain are more like mediaeval neumes (an ancient way of putting down the sounds of plainchant for the monastic offices). These neumes stand for the quiet, insistent Word of God. It is like being held in the gaze of someone whose voice you cannot ignore.

Selecting elements for the work

The neume shapes themselves have a rock-like surface. They rise out of darkness, lit with a central, gentle golden glow. There is nothing forceful or aggressive about this Logos, this personification of God's Word. It is solid, enduring, eternal.

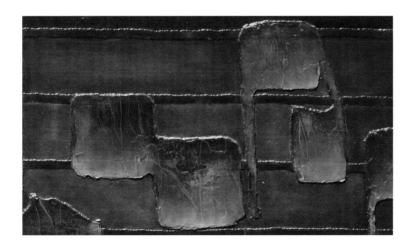

# THE CHILDREN OF GOD

To all those who have received him,
the Word has given the power
to become children of God. And God has sent
into their heart the Spirit of his Son, crying:
'Abba! Father!'

And so we rise –
We scraps of hope and bone
Are gathered,
Aligned by sinew and desire
To cry for, to breathe our All,
Our Abba.

In this truth we stay,
As Spirit spreads her cloak
Over the bare soul's flesh,
And rocks the crib of our content.

The sky is cavernous
And creation sighs,
Its clay also, a bed
For cherishing.

This image began with a series of happy accidents. The week before I was intending to start work on this fifth piece, I was out walking with my daughter Abigail, and our dog Holly. We took a new route through fields we often use and came across a piece of weathered and broken trellis. I picked it up and put it in one of the carrier bags I always take with me on walks, 'just in case'. Later that week, I was experimenting with some of the copper pieces and discovered that I could dramatically change the surface by applying various materials to the metal while very hot. (I probably broke several health and safety recommendations by heating the copper on my gas cooker at home.) As a result, I managed to create intriguing tones and shapes on a rectangular piece of copper that would be perfect for what I was beginning to imagine in my mind's eye.

Sarah said that she saw a sea of orange when she played this movement. Orange is a mixture of red and yellow, and in Kandinsky's theory of colour, red is 'alive, restless, constantly striving towards a goal' while for yellow he gives the colour the instrumental voice of a 'fanfare of high trumpets'. Certainly the musical beginning of 'The Children of God' is an urgent, passionate ascent to its climactic crescendo. You can clearly hear the upward clambering. The newly discovered wooden trellis seemed the perfect 'found object' to describe it. Of course, the trellis is fractured and fragile but that is entirely appropriate for describing humanity's striving efforts that so often involve times of failure as a necessary opportunity for greater self-understanding. At the start of this book is a photo of my sculpture carrying the gilded words, 'For when I am weak, then I am strong.' This quote from Paul's letter to the Corinthians is ex-

tremely important to me. It demonstrates that our

vulnerability is, paradoxically, the very thing that can bring us strength. This way of living may run counter to the 'natural' but it is what Christ embodied in his passion. So the fragile, broken piece of wood I used in this work can at the same time symbolize the power and energy humanity receives in responding to God's call.

The copper becomes the heart of the Father to whom the children are calling. From this glowing rectangle comes bright light that touches on the tips of the tumbling structure climbing towards it.

Behind the trellis and copper is a complex layering of turquoise and oranges. Turquoise, as well as a beautiful colour in its own right, is also an admixture of green and blue. Green is used in icons for Creation, and often also to represent the Holy Spirit (such as in Rublev's spectacular 'Hospitality of Abraham'). Blue, as I've mentioned earlier, evokes divine nature. Combining the two colours in this and other images brings the two meanings together. The image is neither confined to earth, nor to an event in heaven, but is somehow in either or both spheres.

Background colours and horizons

There's also a theological link with the turquoise of 'Eternal Designs'– as God's eternal purposes for creation are being fulfilled in making us Children of God.

Multi-coloured metallic threads make further horizon lines, some of which are highlighted with a touch of gold or iridescence.

I picked out the rising horizon in washes of burnt sienna and cadmiums, and below is a softly textured band, almost like ruddy-coloured soil from which the whole image seems to grow. It relates to a quiet musical phrase towards the end of this movement, where everything feels calm and secure.

# THE ANGELS

The multitude of the heavenly host,
praising God and saying:
Glory to God in the Highest.

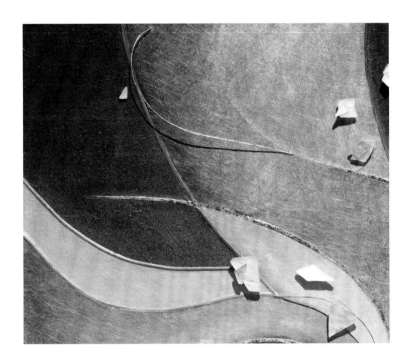

Poised on frosted wing,
Pure spirits glint, alive in light,
And slip through heaven's glass.

The host of God's messengers arrive:
In haste, expectantly, like birds
They swarm; they dive and wheel in awe:
'He is born!' they thrill.

Scintillant,
Spiralling, they circle low
To kiss the furrowed land
And chatter its repair.

To praise again they soar,
Hover high in upper air,
Twist, and disappear.

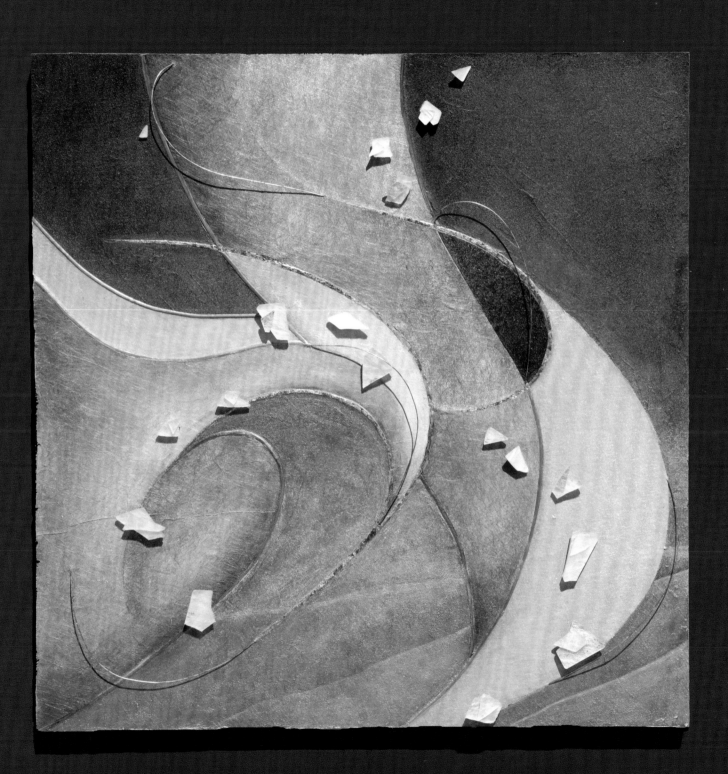

Starlings in flight

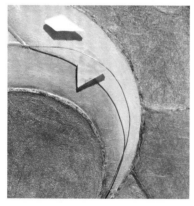

Gilded wire and covered perspex fragment

The starting point for this image came from a comment by Sarah, when she likened the swirling musical shapes of 'The Angels' to the flight of a flock of starlings.

I was lucky enough to find a short piece of film in which huge swarms of these tiny dynamos exploded out of the ground and whirled between copses of trees, over ploughed fields, covering vast expanses of sky in moments. I drew dozens of sketches from this film, trying to find a composition that would achieve balance and movement at the same time. I eventually settled on the simplified shapes used in this image.

The next challenge was to find a surface texture that would evoke the softness of angel wings, without being descriptively literal. By happy chance, I found just what I needed in a tiny craft shop in Salisbury. This open weave material, once applied to the panel, was glazed in blues and greens, with touches of transparent white and iridescent medium. Unfortunately the relatively small amount this craft shop was able to supply wasn't enough for the whole image, so a frantic search of alternative outlets began. I never succeeded in finding exactly the same material, which had been obtained from a now-defunct supplier in Germany, but I found alternatives that provided interesting contrasts of tone and texture, and perhaps was all the better for that.

A satisfyingly therapeutic part of making 'The Angels' was smashing sheets of mirrored Perspex with a mallet, to create random, sparkly highlights. I covered the resulting shards with a delicate filigree fabric and built them into the image, supported from beneath by large felting nails. These shards perform two functions. First, by attaching them at random, tipping angles from the surface of the panel, they reflect light in unexpected ways, adding movement and activity. Second, they help

42

to bring the image forward, into our space. One of the surprisingly difficult tasks was to place these in a way that didn't feel too random, but had some purpose without being formally patterned.

Unfortunately it has proved difficult to get a true photograph of the particular qualities and colour in this image, because there is so much sparkle and shimmer.

Strong flexible wires were gilded with a beautiful mottled metallic leaf that has something of the look of mother-of-pearl. Once I embedded the wires into the supporting panel, they could lift out of the surface, emphasizing and echoing the curves that make up the main shapes. The shadows cast by these wires are intrinsic to the design, and change shape and direction as the viewer's gaze moves across the surface. Some of the main forms in the design are made from narrow strips of lead; in the context of this image, perhaps lead's association with stained glass might be a more appropriate one than the passion, though that resonance would still be there, even at the moment of Christ's birth. Other curves have been built up with gesso and then gilded like the wires with the same pearly metallic leaf.

The angels rise up from the furrowed land and rich with gold, as if the very earth becomes precious and glorious as it witnesses this ecstatic burst of joy. Again, just over the horizon is a glint of dawn as the angels herald a spectacular new beginning.

'The furrowed land'

43

# JESUS ACCEPTS SUFFERING

Christ said to his Father on entering the world:
'You have no pleasure in either burnt offerings
or sacrifices for sin, but you have prepared
a body for me. Here I am!'

Heavy on earth,
The weight of Justice falls,
Harsh and terrible.

But a Body replies:
His ears hear in splintered right a call,
Hands clasp what is knotted and gnarled
And play against the grain of wrong;
Hence the world's wood is turned:

He takes the cross eternally,
And fixes it with love.

The demand
Becomes a door,
A stair on which to rise
To bear up blood in triumph.

Central beam, rising beyond the top edge of the panel

In the Introduction, I mention that it can sometimes take years before I know how or where I'm going to use a particular material or found object. This was the case with the central beam of 'Jesus Accepts Suffering'. It is a large piece of driftwood I found many years ago, deeply weathered and very thick, complete with rusted nails. It might have been part of a roof beam.

Several times it nearly became part of a larger sculpture, but was just too intriguing and engaging not to be centre stage. The beam represents two things – it is Christ's acceptance, and at the same time the cross of crucifixion. The dark painted panel, cut through and placed either side of the beam is almost like the flesh of Christ, which has opened up to accept this insistent and demanding wood. Then it becomes incorporated, echoing the lines and colours singing out from the darkness. I began this image with a dense layer of pure graphite on the panels, a glorious mineral pigment that has an almost metallic sheen to it. It is also deeply, intensely dark, without quite becoming black. Graphite is not a true grey, but is a colour in its own right. Greys are never used in the lexicon of icon palettes. They are produced by mixing black (representing sin or injustice) and white (signifying righteousness). In the language of icons, this then becomes a 'non-colour' – an almost non-existence. I like the symbolism of a colour meaning 'absence'. It also seems appropriate for aspects of this particular image.

Over the graphite are transparent glazes of colour. Greens and yellows recall the colours of Christ's flesh and 'corrupted Creation'. Grünewald uses colours like these in his crucifixion for the Isenheim Altarpiece.

Detail of Grünewald's 'Isenheim Altarpiece'

There are other colours as well, including those described earlier for their relevance in sacred art: blues, reds and the same very finely ground gold used in 'Eternal Designs'. The effect of glazing over a dark background gives the colours an ephemeral quality, like a draped sheer fabric caught in a slight breeze. This effect could describe the curtain of the temple torn in two at the moment when Christ breathes his last on the cross.

Running the length of the top of the image is a strongly textured section. It could be read as a cross-beam but I mean it to express the feeling of a downward, oppressive weight, devoid of the luminosity of the lower part.

The narrow lines of lead form a sort of linear cross, laid down at an acute angle and using a type of inverse perspective. This is another technique often used in icons, which reverses the effect of single-point perspective (that of creating a convincing sense of visual depth in an image), encouraging the viewer to participate in the sacred scene.

The music for 'Jesus Accepts Suffering' begins with dark and minor notes of suffering, but ends with a transformative, triumphant chord. Allowing the beam to break free from the constraints of the square panel reflects the Christian perspective that suffering and sorrow are not the final word on any story.

Glazing the panel

Close-up of lead, oblique view of beam

# THE MAGI

The Magi departed
and the star went before them.

The cavalcade sways unerring
Across the sleeping earth –
Red, blue, green, processing –
Crowned with purple overhead.

One simple thought unites them:
To follow wherever casts
The star its silver thread
And maps their elemental way.

But how will they arrive
And taste Christ's promised rest?

Only by slowing to the state
Where selves are bowed and stilled
And the hours soft and stretched
By dawn's bright Majesty.

The great organ at Winchester Cathedral, where the project began

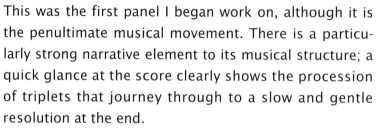

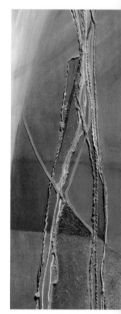

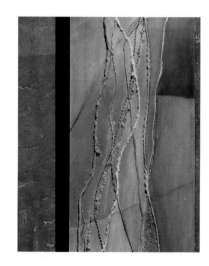

This was the first panel I began work on, although it is the penultimate musical movement. There is a particularly strong narrative element to its musical structure; a quick glance at the score clearly shows the procession of triplets that journey through to a slow and gentle resolution at the end.

The triplet structure hints at the traditional reading of there being three magi, the 'Three Wise Men'. It is unlikely that these magi were kings. Perhaps they were members of a priestly caste. There is also no clear evidence of how many made the journey across the Syrian Desert, but historically it is assumed there were three, because three gifts are mentioned. Early Christian art doesn't offer a firm number, with a variety of paintings and frescos depicting two, three, four and eight, and in some Oriental traditions as many as twelve.

As this was my first panel, I decided to pay an initial homage to the cathedral organ by using strong, simple upright forms, like organ pipes. I also felt that these three characters needed to have authority and a sense of the regal, and the resolutely vertical lines seemed to emphasize that.

Behind the formal figures are colours of a desert sky at night, which become undulating patterns of sand and cloud, bathed in royal blues and purples. The rising horizon already mentioned in various other works is also discreetly present.

The magi themselves are wrapped in shimmery threads matched to their respective colour harmony, of either red, blue or green. As with 'The Virgin and Child' the threads imply clothing for the characters in the image. In designing the patterns of colour, I had most strongly in mind the nature of their journey. The star had taken them away from what and where they knew, into the unknown and as yet unrevealed. I imagined crudely drawn maps, gulleys and crevasses through mountain and desert that had to be negotiated. I could also see the folds of their robes buffeted about in wind and sandstorm. My aim was to bring some of that imagery to the way I handled the paint, to bring flow and movement into these otherwise rather rigid, stately forms.

An encounter with God can be intense, personal and all-consuming, as it was for Mary. It can be sudden, almost alarming, a great shout into our normal, quiet pattern of life, as with the shepherds. It can also be found at the end of a long, considered journey. This was the experience for the magi. They didn't know what the eventual reward would be, but willing to take the risk, they discovered greater riches than those they had brought with them.

# GOD AMONG US

Words of the communicant, of the Virgin,
of the whole Church: He who created me
has rested in my tabernacle, the Word
was made flesh and dwelt in me.
My soul magnifies the Lord and my spirit
has rejoiced in God my Saviour.

To pitch his tent among us
Our Creator comes, mighty
To the fabric he has made,
To bind its ancient tears.

Sharing in the substance that is ours
To bring the Fire which is his –
That incandescence of his very self –
To raise us daughters, sons of God.

What unjust exchange, and yet well fair.

So let carnival begin –
A dazzling whirligig of joy,
Of which all redounds
From his crashing descent
As Man.

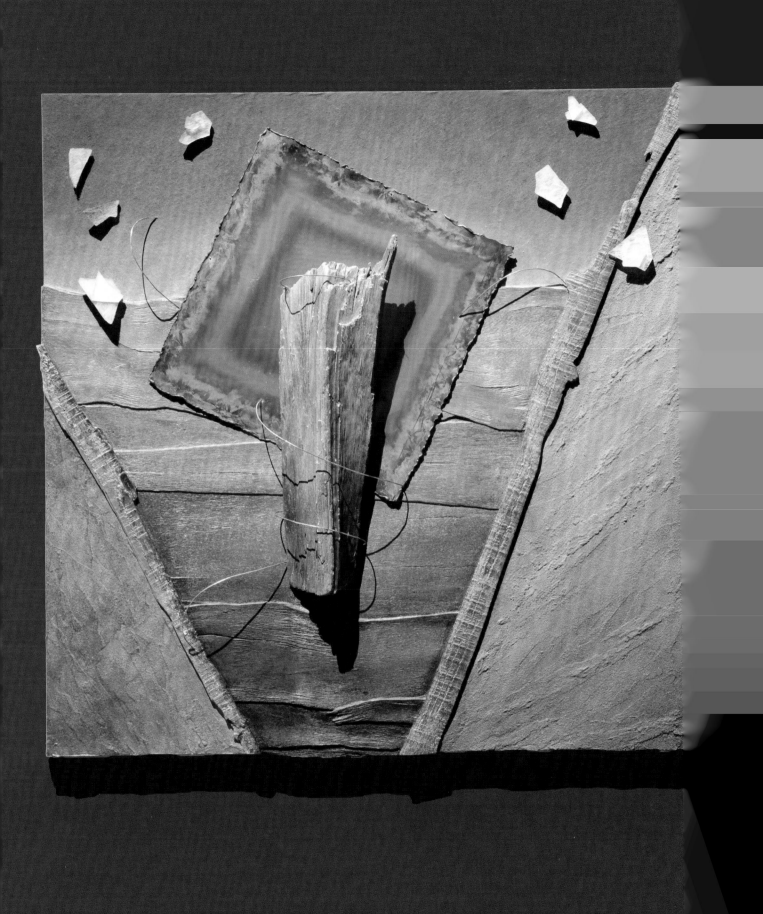

The final piece. It would have been impossible to make this one until I had completed all of the previous eight, because Messiaen makes musical references to most – if not all – of the earlier themes in this last great, shattering crescendo. I can hear particularly the presence of 'The Word' and the yearning strains of the 'Children of God', but there are certainly other movements in evidence. I wanted to make reference to materials and colours used in the earlier eight works. Sarah and I worked closely on the initial ideas for the composition, and we began with a dominating V shape, whose point dips so deeply down that it isn't even included in the panel. Here is the sense that when God comes to meet us as we are, there are no depths to which he will not travel:

> For I am convinced that neither death, nor life, nor angels, nor rulers, nor things present, nor things to come, nor powers, nor height, nor depth, nor anything else in all creation, will be able to separate us from the love of God in Christ Jesus our Lord.
>
> (Romans 8.38–39)

The downward V is made from slivers of rough-sawn wood, gilded with a metallic leaf full of colours, similar to that used in 'The Angels'. The area immediately below it is gilded with copper leaf, then burnished and glazed over with more colours.

Complemented on the other side is the upward arm of the V, the striving hope we find also in 'The Children of God'. I've used similar textures and colours in this area of the image as in that fifth panel.

The space between this central V is bridged by a surface that takes us straight back to the stable, with the same simple wooden paneling, though here with different tones. The colour is more built up, with washes of crimson, rose, ultramarine, and royal purple, then rubbed over with iridescent white.

An ancient piece of oak, symbolizing both the incarnation and the cross, rises straight out of the stable and up from the deepest point of the V. This is the heart of the whole composition. The top edge of the oak is worn and weathered into a kind of crown.

There is a glow below the base of the oak and reaching to the lowest edge of the panel. It is almost like a shadow, but one made of light rather than the absence of light.

In traditional icons there are no painted shadows, because everything in creation is suffused by the light of God, which is all around and equally dispersed. There are also no painted shadows in these nine works, although inevitably, the objects and textures cast actual shadows, which vary and move as the light around them changes.

A large square of highly polished copper sits behind the central form, full of colours created by the heat of the gas flame that cut it. Unlike the other square and rectangular forms in this series, it sits on neither a vertical nor horizontal line. Instead it tips at an unresolved angle, giving a slightly unsettling quality to the composition. The copper, with its intense response to light, represents the presence of God and the eternal realm.

Angels flit and spin across the surface, bright with joy. The sky drops down behind the horizon, and there, once again, is the gleam of dawn beyond the horizon.

Angels flit across the impending dawn

# CONCLUSION

Nine months after beginning the first of these pieces the studio work was complete, an appropriate timespan to develop ideas around the Incarnation! The premiere at Winchester Cathedral, in Messiaen's centenary year, led to a programme of further outings for the project, which has been very exciting and rewarding.

My aim was to draw deeply on the theology of the Incarnation, which is at the heart of every movement in *La Nativité du Seigneur*. I've been challenged to consolidate a new visual language, not just for the individual pieces, but in seeing all nine of them work together as a whole. Perhaps most significant has been the opportunity to focus on the use of found materials and give them unashamedly incarnational meanings: Christ's strong, yet broken body can be represented in the simplest fragments of creation (such as the crumb of a communion wafer). I've also become clearer about the links between my own style of work and traditional aspects of religious art, including the theological language of colour and sacred geometry.

For nine months, I listened repeatedly to the music of Messiaen, often in the very small hours of morning when everything else was utterly quiet – a time I find particularly inspiring to work in. It was strange to return to silence when the work had left the studio. It felt empty in more ways than one. I'm sure I will work again with music as inspiration, either directly or implicitly. For the moment, I am choosing to work in silence, continuing to experiment with colours and some new materials, and also making larger-scale sculptures.

I have begun work on a series of sculptures based on Christ's Passion, a variant of the 'Stations of the Cross'. I hope to complete this by the spring of 2010. In the meantime, I shall be out beachcombing, collecting inspiring junk and finding excuses to take the dog for long walks, always with a backpack or bag handy just in case of interesting finds.